YOUR KNOWLEDGE HAS VALUE

Natural Evil, Suffering, a New Encyclical and a New World Order. A Socio-Religious Perspective on the Spirit of "Fratelli Tutti"

Tarcisius Mukuka

GRIN

Bibliographic information published by the German National Library:

The German National Library lists this publication in the National Bibliography; detailed bibliographic data are available on the Internet at http://dnb.dnb.de.

ISBN: 9783346340962
This book is also available as an ebook.

© GRIN Publishing GmbH
Nymphenburger Straße 86
80636 München

Print and binding: Books on Demand GmbH, Norderstedt, Germany
Printed on acid-free paper from responsible sources.

The present work has been carefully prepared. Nevertheless, authors and publishers do not incur liability for the correctness of information, notes, links and advice as well as any printing errors.

GRIN web shop: https://www.grin.com/document/968823

Natural Evil, Suffering, a New Encyclical and a New World Order
A Socio-Religious Perspective on the Spirit of *Fratelli Tutti*

By Dr Tarcisius Mukuka
Kwame Nkrumah University, Kabwe, Zambia

Contents

1. Introduction

This article draws out what my friend Josephine Shamwana-Lungu referred to as the "Spirit of *Fratelli Tutti*" — a spirit of fraternity, solidarity, social friendship and subsidiarity, from the recent encyclical by Pope Francis. I provide a socio-religious or theological perspective on this new encyclical which is a call to humanity to unite and to build a brave new world order after the Covid-19 pandemic. I have limited myself to examining why the encyclical has been well-received (reception of *Fratelli Tutti*), how Covid-19 calls us to a new way of being human (New bottles for new wine and God's possibility in a post Covid-19 Era) in which humanity is being challenged not to return to business as usual in the way we deal with each other; how natural evil, such as a pandemic, cannot thwart the plan of the creator; how the new encyclical factors into a new World Order (*Fratelli Tutti* and a new world order "thanks" to Covid-19), whether God suffers or not, the end point of evolution (Natural evil, suffering, the cost of evolution and the Christic Omega Point) and ending with five lessons I was able to cull from *Fratelli Tutti* (Five takeaways from *Fratelli Tutti*). Written, as the Pope says, when "the Covid-19 pandemic unexpectedly erupted, exposing our false securities" (Pope Francis, *Fratelli Tutti* 2020: par 7). I use that as a jumping off point to challenge the age-old *theologoumenon* of the impassibility of God. I argue that God in fact does suffer as he has been suffering through the ages, even during the Covid-19 pandemic as part of the cost of evolution but he is not overwhelmed by suffering. Natural evil and suffering are par for the course. They are the birth pangs of a new heaven and a new earth. *Fratelli Tutti* calls for a new way of relating to each other as our brothers' and sisters' keepers, as we head towards the Omega Point, to use Pierre Teilhard de Chardin's signature theory.

2. Two Initial Appreciations of *Fratelli Tutti*

Christine Allen, Director of *CAFOD* [Catholic Agency for Overseas Development], with its Head Office at Romero House, 55 Westminster Bridge Road in London, puts her finger on the socio-religious challenge of a pandemic such as Covid-19. She opines that the new papal encyclical by Pope Francis, *Fratelli Tutti*[1] is a "radical blueprint for a post-coronavirus world."[2] The encyclical offers a "vision for real and lasting change, by calling on us to build community at all levels — personal, societal and global, where walls of fear and distrust are replaced by a 'culture of encounter' and our solidarity with others restores human dignity."[3] That, in a nutshell, is the spirit of *Fratelli Tutti*. It is about the kind of initiatives *CAFOD* has been promoting all along in campaigning "for global [and planetary] justice, so that every woman, man and child can live a full and dignified life."[4] According to Pope Francis, it is this "culture of encounter" or what the Brazilian poet, lyricist, essayist and playwright, Vinicius de Moraes, referred to as the "art of encounter" [Portuguese: *arte do encontro*],[5] which will spur us to build what the title of this article optimistically refers to, tongue-in-cheek, as a "brave new world order" as in the dystopian social science fiction novel by English author Aldous Huxley (1932), set in a futuristic World State, whose citizens are environmentally engineered into an intelligence-based social hierarchy. If Aldous Huxley were to allow me, I would add the word emotion after intelligence.

For Cardinal John Dew, Vice-president of New Zealand's Catholic Bishops' Conference, the spirit of *Fratelli Tutti* "is an invitation for everyone to broaden our perspective to view a world without borders and to view every single person on the planet, and yes, the planet itself, as brother and sister"[6] as St Francis reminded us in the Canticle of the Sun.[7] If this sounds Utopian [an imaginary state of affairs in which everything is perfect], it is because we are not there yet. *Fratelli Tutti*, as a roadmap to Utopia, is one way to phrase the argument of this article. Written during the Covid-19 pandemic, *Fratelli Tutti* challenges our theology of natural evil and suffering. I borrow this insight from the late Australian theologian Denis Edwards who argues that "Only a theology of the resurrection that is eschatologically transformative can begin to respond to the suffering that is built into an evolutionary universe" (Edwards 2006b: 817). While we draw breath this side of the Jordan, the keys to making that possible are in *Fratelli Tutti*: fraternity, solidarity, social friendship and subsidiarity through the art of encounter. I think the Jesuits already intuited this, a long time ago, by the formation of Christian Life Community (CLC) which forms a sort of preamble for this analysis of *Fratelli Tutti*.

3. Christian Life Community as *Fratelli Tutti* in Action

According to the CLC website, Christian Life Community is a global association of Christian men and women, adults and young people, of all social conditions, who, inspired by the life and teaching of St Ignatius of Loyola who want to be disciples of Jesus Christ more closely and work with Him for the building of the Kingdom of God — a kingdom of peace, love and justice. The genius of CLC was to intuit that "small is beautiful" by having members make up small groups but these small groups or cells are not insular or narcissistic. They form part of larger communities organised regionally and nationally, all forming one World Community. That is why CLC is present in all five continents, in more than sixty countries. As for its Ignatian ethos, I will let the website speak for itself. The spirituality is uncannily like the spirit of *Fratelli Tutti*.

> The charism and spirituality of CLC are Ignatian. Thus, the Spiritual Exercises of St Ignatius are both the specific source of our charism and the characteristic instrument of CLC spirituality. The CLC way of life is shaped by the features of Ignatian Christology: austere and simple, in solidarity with the poor and the outcasts of society, integrating contemplation and action, in all things living lives of love and service within the Church, always in a spirit of discernment.[8]

I will let Manuel Martínez Arteaga express the CLC spirit which, as my friend Josephine Shamwana-Lungu says, is the "spirit of *Fratelli Tutti*" I have been harping on. Writing in *Progressio*, Manuel Martínez Arteaga reminds us, "Now, let's talk about the latest embrace in these recent times. It is a type of embrace which takes on many forms, but which shares a common feature: it is a virtual or spiritual hug. Many of our national communities are living through the effects of the Covid-19 epidemic. Many of us have had to celebrate our World CLC Day on March 25 through the celebrations of the Eucharist on social networks. These community meetings are happening through different internet platforms, often through methods that we are not accustomed to using. However, this is a time that has awakened in us our creativity, our drive for community, our desire to be present and take care of each other, even at a distance. It has become a time to rediscover the important things inside our hearts, and to realize that despite the individual circumstances which we are all experiencing, we can all fill our days with deep meaning, and with a prayer that carries trust and hope: we shall embrace again."[9] If I was to tweak this message, my exhortation, pandemic or not is to keep embracing, virtually, spiritually or otherwise. That is one way to apply the message of *Fratelli Tutti* and to breathe its spirit.

4. Reception of *Fratelli Tutti* thanks to Covid-19 and a Papal Ideological Manifesto

The "thanks" to Covid-19 in the subtitle is tinged with a hint of sarcasm. But much less than the blessing, miracle, or gift that President Donald Trump attributed to Covid-19 when he posted a video on Twitter saying, "I want everybody to be given the same treatment as your President. Because I feel great, I feel perfect. I think this was a blessing from God that I caught it. This was a blessing in disguise. I caught it, I heard about this drug, I said, let me take it and it was incredible the way it worked. I think if I didn't catch it, we'd be looking at that [*remdesivir*] like a number of other drugs but it really did a fantastic job. I want to get for you what I got and I'm going to make it free."[10] The Covid-19 pandemic, as a form of natural evil has been terrible in its devastation — 37, 423,660 confirmed cases, 1,074,817 confirmed deaths in 235 countries, areas or territories at the time of writing[11] — but the Pope's point in issuing *Fratelli Tutti* is to say that even evil, such as Covid-19, is capable of teaching humanity a few lessons on the future of our planet and of humanity. This article summarises and draws out a socio-religious perspective on the new encyclical by Pope Francis. This is truly a universal letter — to all people of good will — challenging humanity to be the best it can be, "thanks" to the Covid-19 pandemic. Its reception has been universally positive barring a few dissenting voices. What's there to disagree about *Fratelli Tutti*? I wonder.

Anna Rowlands, a British theologian invited to be part of the unveiling of the document at the Vatican, told *Catholic News Service* that the text's "golden thread" is about discerning "what gives life" and "helps everyone to develop their full potential and flourish." Commenting on *Fratelli Tutti*'s second chapter, a stranger on the road, in particular, she says, "When people ask, 'Who is my neighbour?' Often what they really want to know is, "Who is not my neighbour?" or "Who can I legitimately say is not my responsibility?" In contrast, she says the teaching in the document "helps everyone to develop their full potential and flourish."[12]

The Czechoslovakian-born Canadian Cardinal, Jesuit Michael Czerny, put it this way, "You could take a distance from the encyclical and say, 'The Pope is trying to get us to recognize that all these people are our brothers and sisters.' But it's more than that. What he's saying is, 'You've got to be a brother and sister to everyone who needs us.' The category isn't out there; the category is here. Our human family and our common home needs me to be brother to the people who need me and needs you to be sister to these people."[13] I am my brother's and my sister's keeper.

Samuel Gregg, representing the dissenting voice, is less enthusiastic, calling *Fratelli Tutti* a "familiar mixture of dubious claims, strawmen, and genuine insights."[14] Samuel Gregg's critique of the Pope's economic message is blinkered and misses the point of an encyclical. "Also, insufficient — and, alas, this has characterised Francis' pontificate from its very beginning — is *Fratelli Tutti*'s treatment of economic questions," he argues, "It seems that, no matter how many people (not all of whom can be characterised as fiscal conservatives) highlight the economic caricatures that roam throughout Francis' documents, a pontificate which prides itself on its commitment to dialogue just isn't interested in a serious conversation about economic issues outside a very limited circle."[15] This article begs to differ because it understands an encyclical's purpose as exhortative. The Pope is not writing as an economist — he is no Amartya Sen — but a theologian and a pastor.

Larry Chapp, retired professor of theology at DeSales University in Pennsylvania, is more guarded but as he confesses, "Those who know me well understand that I am not generally a fan of Pope Francis, who was elected to reform the Curia (so we are told) but has failed miserably so far in that regard. He has also appointed to high office individuals who seem like old guard, unreconstructed, post Vatican II liberals — which is a bad thing in my view."[16] Having read the encyclical several times, I see no evidence of "Pope Francis' encyclical" suffering "in places with the kind of ambiguities this papacy has all too often engaged in. But it is not, despite what some critics claim, in any way 'heretical' or even 'dangerous.'"[17] I am not sure what's so wrong with his "post Vatican II liberals" apart from being Larry Chapp's own strawmen. And if you are Donald Trump, an encyclical that smells of socialism may well be "heretical" or even "dangerous."

As is to be expected, Carlo Maria Viganò's reaction has been the most vitriolic or malicious. Here is part of his reaction, first in Italian, followed by my translation in square brackets. "Ad una lettura cursoria del testo dell'enciclica *Fratelli tutti* si sarebbe indotti a credere che essa sia stata scritta da un massone, non dal Vicario di Cristo. Tutto quanto vi è contenuto è ispirato ad un vago deismo e ad un filantropismo che non ha nulla di cattolico: *Nonne et ethnici hoc faciunt? Non fanno così anche i pagani?* (Mt 5.47)"[18] [At a cursory reading of the text of the encyclical *Fratelli Tutti*, one would be led to believe that it was written by a Mason, not by the Vicar of Christ. Everything in it is inspired by a vague deism and a philanthropism that has nothing Catholic in it: *Nonne et ethnici hoc faciunt?* Do not even the pagans do the same? (Mt 5.47)]. His conclusion is: "Questa Enciclica costituisce il manifesto ideologico di Bergoglio — la sua *Professio fidei masonicae* — e la sua candidatura alla presidenza della Religione Universale, ancella del Nuovo Ordine Mondiale. Tanta attestazione di subalternità[19] al pensiero mainstream gli potrà forse valere il plauso dei nemici di Dio, ma conferma l'inesorabile abbandono della missione evangelizzatrice della Chiesa. D'altra parte, l'abbiamo già udito: 'Il proselitismo è una solenne sciocchezza'"[20] [This Encyclical constitutes Bergoglio's ideological manifesto — his *Professio fidei masonicae* — and his candidacy for the presidency of Universal Religion, handmaid of the New World Order. Such attestation of subalternity[21] to mainstream thought may perhaps be worth the applause of the enemies of God, but it confirms the inexorable abandonment of the evangelising mission of the Church. On the other hand, we have already heard it: 'Proselytism is solemn nonsense'].

Proselytism, solemn nonsense? Did Pope Francis really say that? I am afraid he did and I think he meant it, when he spoke to the founder of Italian newspaper, *La Repubblica*, Eugenio Scalfari. Proselytism wreaks of forced conversions and is everything that evangelisation is not. Pope Francis was right not to touch Proselytism with a badge pole. This is how Eugenio Scalfari reports part of the encounter. "The Pope comes in and shakes my hand, and we sit down. The Pope smiles and says: 'Some of my colleagues who know you told me that you will try to convert me.' It's a joke, I tell him. My friends think it is you who wants to convert me. He smiles again and replies: 'Proselytism is solemn nonsense, it makes no sense. We need to get to know each other, listen to each other and improve our knowledge of the world around us. Sometime after our meeting I want to arrange another one because new ideas are born and I discover new needs. This is important: to get to know people, listen, expand the circle of ideas. The world is crisscrossed by roads that come closer together and move apart, but the important thing is that they lead towards the Good."[22] But it was Eugenio Scalfaro's conclusion that ties this interview with the spirit of *Fratelli Tutti*, "We shake hands and he stands with his two fingers raised in a blessing. I wave to him from the window. This is Pope Francis. If the Church becomes what he thinks and wishes it to be, an epoch will have changed [*Se la Chiesa diventerà come lui la pensa e la vuole sarà cambiata un'epoca*]."[23] If the world listens to *Fratelli Tutti*, or as my friend Josephine Shamwana-Lungu told me recently, adopts the "spirit of *Fratelli Tutti*,"[24] surely, "it will be an epochal change."[25] But before that happens, there would need to be "new bottles for new wine" or "new wine into fresh wineskins" (Mark 2.21–22 *NRSV*). The Palestinian Rabbi's socio-economic world was as epochal as the one we are living in, pandemic or not. As Pope Francis pointed out in *Fratelli Tutti*, "Anyone who thinks that the only lesson to be learned was the need to improve what we were already doing, or to refine existing systems and regulations, is denying reality" (*Fratelli Tutti* 2020: par 8).

5. New Bottles for New Wine and God's Passibility in a Post Covid-19 Era

Does God suffer? Has God been suffering during the Covid-19 pandemic, to take a current specific instance? This is a theological conundrum I hope to attempt to answer here. But first, Julian Huxley's metaphor, which I adopt here, "new bottles for new wine" (Huxley 1951), is clearly an update and a variation on the Synoptic Gospel metaphor, first used by the Palestinian Rabbi, "new wine into fresh wineskins." Mark reports Jesus teaching that "No one sews a piece of unshrunk cloth on an old cloak; otherwise, the patch pulls away from it, the new from the old, and a worse tear is made. And no one puts new wine into old wineskins; otherwise, the wine will burst the skins, and the wine is lost, and so are the skins; but one puts new wine into fresh wineskins" (Mark 2.21–22 *NRSV*).

James Edwards' comment on the above two short parables helps us to appreciate what is going on in our own times as we stand on the verge of a post Covid-19 era which we seem to agree for a change that this cannot be a return to business as usual. The phrase "new normal" makes the same point. "The question posed by the image of the wedding feast and the two atom-like parables is not whether disciples will, like sewing a new patch on an old garment or refilling an old container, make room for Jesus in their already full agendas [sic] and lives. The question is whether they will forsake business as usual and join the wedding celebration; whether they will become entirely new receptacles for the expanding fermentation of Jesus and the Gospel in their lives" (Edwards 2002: 92). In a post Covid-19 era, the question is whether our society and Church structures can become "entirely new receptacles for the expanding fermentation of Jesus and the Gospel" (Edwards 2002: 92) in our lives. In Pope Francis' case, the starting point was the Vatican itself, as in the smallest sovereign state. Just a year after his election, *BBC News* reported that "Pope Francis has dismissed the entire board of the Vatican's financial regulator as he looks to reform the city-state's banking practices following a corruption scandal. The move is also reportedly due to infighting among the 'old guard.' The Financial Intelligence Authority's Italian, five-person board were due to see their terms expire in 2016. They are being replaced with four international experts from Italy, Singapore, Switzerland and the US. The Vatican said the new directors include Juan Zarate, a former national security adviser to US President George Bush, and Joseph Pillay, a civil servant and adviser to the president of Singapore. The other two board members are Maria Bianca Farina, an executive at the Italian postal service and Marc Odendall, a Swiss financial consultant."[26] Becoming "entirely new receptacles for the expanding fermentation of Jesus and the Gospel" (Edwards 2002: 92) in the life of the planet and of humanity is the challenge that faced Pope Francis as he reflected on what lessons Covid-19 could teach us.

I now want to place the insights of the new encyclical in the context of natural evil, which is what any pandemic is. As far as I am aware, none of the commentators on *Fratelli Tutti* are taking on this conundrum. Part of the problem is that most theological reflections on natural evil suffer from one Achilles Heel. They are married to the doctrine of the impassibility of God and I am not, especially as a biblical scholar who has to explain a God who gets upset, changes his mind and is even described as jealous. "Roughly, the impassibility thesis is the claim that God does not undergo sensory experience including suffering and pain, nor is God subject to corruption, substantial essential change or to external agency" (Taliaferro 1989: 217). It has often been seen as a consequence of divine *aseity*, whereby "God is accordingly absolutely self-sufficient, depending upon nothing outside of himself, but purely moved by his own will" (Peckham 2012: 91–92). The doctrines of God's *aseity* and impassibility raise the theological conundrum of natural evil, such as Covid-19 and how they square up in God's loving plan and omnipotence for the planet and for humanity which will be dealt with in the course of this article. I think the problem with the impassibility and *aseity* doctrines is that they suffer from literal anthropomorphism. Literal anthropomorphism is the simplest form of anthropomorphism, referring to when something is understood literally as acting like a human being. This is the premise of fairy tales when trees and animals speak. Metaphorical anthropomorphism, which I think applies to the Bible and theology

7

and is a case of personification. It makes the point that something is like something else. What literal anthropomorphism forgets is that when A is like B, it is also true that A is not like B. This is clearly the case with theological anthropomorphism. If A standing for God is like B, humans, it does not follow that this relationship can be presented in the form of an equation A=B. God is sentient, able to suffer or feel but is not overwhelmed by emotion but transcends it. It's time we got over it, God does get upset but does not get unhinged as we do.

6. Natural Evil, Suffering, a New Encyclical and New World Order

I started working on this socio-theological or religious reflection as soon as Vatican spokesperson Matteo Bruni confirmed rumours on Saturday, 5 September 2020 that Pope Francis was set to release a new encyclical on human fraternity. I had no inside knowledge of the content of the new papal encyclical *Fratelli Tutti*. Only the translators did and they were all sworn to pontifical secrecy but if I was a betting man, I would have put my money on contextualising this new encyclical as the fruit of the Pope's meditation on a new world order post Covid-19. As Claire Giangravé wrote in *Religion News Service* on 8 September 2020, "While some people spent the months-long lockdowns making bread, knitting or watching Netflix, Francis seems to have pondered a plan for a new economic model"[27] underpinned by the common good. The choice of the title and launching of the encyclical at Assisi all pointed to a sort of human, global and planetary solidarity new deal. One possible hint what we were to expect from the new encyclical was an interview the Pope gave to the Spanish review *Vida Nueva* [New Life] in April 2020. I highlight one theme, that of solidarity, from the Pope's meditation. First, this is how the *Vida Nueva* sums up the Pope's meditation entitled, *Un Plan Para Resucitar* [A plan to resurrect], followed by the Pope's words.

"The Pope writes in '*Vida Nueva*,' an unpublished reflection for an Easter marked by the coronavirus. Starting from the 'rejoice' of Jesus to women, he affirms the civilisation of love. Francisco calls for getting 'the necessary antibodies of justice, charity and solidarity' for reconstruction on the day after the pandemic. 'It is the Risen One who wants to resurrect all of humanity,' he asserts in this roadmap that the Bishop of Rome gives to the readers of the magazine, to the Church and to society."[28] "At this time, we have realised the importance of 'uniting the entire human family in the search for sustainable and integral development.' Each individual action is not an isolated action, for better or for worse, it has consequences for others, because everything is connected in our common house; and if the health authorities order confinement in homes, it is the people who make it possible, aware of their co-responsibility to stop the pandemic. 'An emergency like Covid-19 is defeated in the first place with the antibodies of solidarity.'"[29]

It is worth noting that Pope Francis' meditation, using metaphors, was a reflection on the good news of Easter, starting with Jesus' greeting to the women who witnessed the resurrection. The *NRSV* says, "Suddenly Jesus met them and said, 'Greetings!'" (Mt 28.9a). I think the imperative "Χαίρετε" [*Chairete*] ought to have been translated "rejoice, be glad, rejoice exceedingly, be well, thrive." The good news the Pope was sharing with us in April 2020 is the same good news we can expect from his new encyclical *Fratelli Tutti*; that we can be whole and healed as humanity only through solidarity by being our brothers' and sisters' keepers. While I hear the arguments, both for keeping and jettisoning the title *Fratelli Tutti*, I was hoping that a last-minute endnote 1 by the translators would put us all out of our misery. Alas, no last-minute endnote 1 by the translators was forthcoming when the encyclical was released on 4 October 2020. Instead endnote 1 turned out to be a reference to *Admonition* VI without any further explanation but in defence of the Pope, nothing in the encyclical wreaks of sexism or gender bias. Even what it says about women cannot be further from mansplaining. If anything, the phrase "brothers and sisters" is used 28 times. *Fratelli Tutti* appears only twice: in the title and the incipit, without translation. Its function is to act as a peg with which to hang the document on the line. On this peg hangs part of the argument of this article that only a positive theology of creation, suffering, possibility of God, theological anthropomorphism, natural evil and what Denis Edwards refers to as "the cost of evolution" (Edwards 2006a; 2006b and 2019) will yield what I am referring to as "a brave new world order."

7. Creation, Covid-19, Natural Evil, Suffering and the Cost of Evolution

But how does natural evil, such as Covid-19, especially the suffering engendered by it, factor in the Pope's encyclical. In two words — a lot. The word suffering or sufferings appears 27 times in the encyclical (par 16, 38, 50, 65x2, 67x2, 68x2, 69, 71, 81, 116, 137, 138, 165, 179, 186x2, 193, 246, 248, 251x2, 253, 274 and 287). Although these 27 instances do not debate how suffering squares up with a loving God or his impassibility, I find that they cohere with Australian theologian Denis Edwards who argues that "Only a theology of the resurrection that is eschatologically transformative can begin to respond to the suffering that is built into an evolutionary universe….A second requirement is that this divine action be understood in a noninterventionist way….The third requirement for a theology of divine action that might offer some response to the costs of evolution would involve an understanding of God's power as constrained by God's love and respect for creatures" (Edwards 2006b: 817). This is the kind of theology and eschatology that Paul grapples with in 1 Corinthians 15. Denis Edwards goes so far as to say that "In such a view of divine power, the love that defines the divine nature is understood as a love that *waits upon* creation, living with its processes, accompanying each creature in love, rejoicing in every emergence, suffering with every suffering creature, and promising to bring all to healing and fullness of life" (Edwards 2006b: 818 — italics in the original). Yes, God suffers with every suffering creature. God has been and is suffering during the Covid-19 pandemic. Denis Edwards has made the same point in "Every Sparrow that Falls to the Ground: The Cost of Evolution and the Christ-Event" (Edwards 2006a). St Paul had grappled much earlier with what Denis Edwards refers to as "a love that *waits upon* creation" in an iconic passage from his letter to the Romans.

"[18] I consider [Λογίζομαι] that the sufferings [παθήματα] of this present time are not worth comparing with the glory [δόξαν] about to be revealed [ἀποκαλυφθῆναι] to us. [19] For the creation waits with eager longing for the revealing of the children of God; [20] for the creation was subjected [ὑπετάγη] to futility [ματαιότητι], not of its own will but by the will of the one who subjected it,

9

in hope [21] that the creation itself will be set free [ἐλευθερωθήσεται] from its bondage [δουλείας] to decay [φθορᾶς] and will obtain the freedom of the glory of the children of God. [22] We know that the whole creation has been groaning [συστενάζει] in labour pains [συνωδίνει] until now; [23] and not only the creation, but we ourselves, who have the first fruits of the Spirit, groan inwardly while we wait for adoption [υἱοθεσίαν], the redemption [ἀπολύτρωσιν] of our bodies. [24] For in hope we were saved. Now hope that is seen is not hope. For who hopes for what is seen? [25] But if we hope for what we do not see, we wait for it with patience" [ὑπομονῆς] (Rom 8.18–25 *NRSV*).

The above words of Paul can be summarised as follows: In v18 we are informed that we suffer now, even from Covid-19, hurricanes and tsunamis. Natural evil is a fact of life but in the grand scheme of things our present troubles are nothing in comparison to the glory that awaits us. This passage tells us that in the future, God will show us our evolved fullness, both as a planet and as human beings. In v19 everything that God created waits eagerly for that evolutionary peak. Then God will reveal the true identity of his children. In v20 the world that God created suffered apparent defeat, as it must have appeared during the Covid-19 pandemic. This was not the fault of the world itself. But God allowed this because there is a future hope built into the DNA of creation, not because he was impassible. In v21 God promised that he would heal the world. God would free the world so it would not end up in futility. He would free the world so that it can share in the wonderful freedom of God's children. In v22 St Paul then tells us that we know how deeply everything suffers. Everything that God created is crying in pain right up to now, pain like the pain of a mother who is giving birth to a child. V23 assures us that the birth pangs are not the end of the story. We ourselves already have the Holy Spirit as a promise of future blessing. But we are crying inside as we wait eagerly for God to adopt us completely as his children after our alienation through natural evil and sin. Then he will free our bodies as he raises them to a new life through the resurrection and bring creation to a full circle because he has suffered in solidarity with the rest of his creation. V24 reminds us that God saved us because we had this hope in our DNA, shot into us at creation like a vaccine. This would not be hope if we had already received these things. Nobody hopes for what he has already, St Paul argues. In v25 we hope for what we do not have already. So, we wait for it patiently. In short, we wait for the resurrection patiently.

Just before he died on 5 March 2019, Australian theologian Denis Edwards, wrote, and this may be a fitting conclusion to this section on "Creation, Covid-19, natural evil, suffering and the cost of evolution" that "If we were simply to observe nature today, in the light of science, and leave aside Christian revelation and other religious beliefs, I think we would need to say that the experience of the natural world is deeply ambiguous. The natural world is unspeakably beautiful, wonderfully bountiful, endlessly fascinating, a place of interconnections and cooperation. But it is also a place of competition, violence, predation, suffering, and death. In this ambiguity, I believe it is the good news of God revealed to us in Jesus that is decisive for Christians. It is not the natural world itself, but the Word made flesh in Jesus that tells us that competition, suffering, and death are not the ultimate meaning of creation. In Jesus, God is revealed as Love that embraces suffering creation, transforming it from within, bringing it to liberation and fulfilment. It is only in Christ, I believe, that we can dare to say that, in the face of the ambiguity we find in the natural world, that Love is the meaning of the whole creation" (Edwards 2019: 31).

I think Italian scholar, Gianfranco Longo, makes a similar point but uses the concept of original sin to underpin his theory of redemption in the face of Jesus' suffering on Calvary. But I think Gianfranco Longo's language is more laboured, even in the original Italian version of the following formulation which I give in translation. "In creating humanity and the world, completed and realised by God, the multiplicity of the form of becoming, the development and transformation of the world and of humanity in the world emerges from an initial reflection. This fact, often glimpsed sociologically as progress, biologically as evolution, etc., is actually characterised by the plurality of phenomena originating from the only possible form from which that whole had its origin and foundation: the faith of God the Father in the love of Jesus for the salvation of the initial *fiat*, a faith to which the Son of God, Jesus, responds through the hope and love of his own immolation, marking Calvary the instant of the New Creation through which Christ re-gives humanity to the world, re-creates and re-composes humanity as a new and redeemed humanity, precisely in the event of love in which Jesus himself gives His Life" (Longo 2013: 17 — my translation).

What Denis Edwards and Gianfranco Longo try to explain about suffering or natural evil was already attempted in Jürgen Moltmann's *The Crucified God*, first published in 1972 when he was professor of theology at the University of Tübingen. Writing in the foreword to the 40th edition of the book, Miroslav Volf had this to say: "This simple and profound thought [of a God who suffers in solidarity with afflicted creatures and redeems them through that suffering] lies at the heart of the book [*The Crucified God*] — difficult and unacceptable to many, especially among trained theologians committed to God's impassibility, and hopeful and comforting to many more, especially among the afflicted, whether they live in fear for life in war torn cities, eke out a miserable existence in shantytowns, wait for death in the cruel belly of prisons, or struggle against an illness eating away their body or soul" (Moltmann 2015: ix) or plucked away by Covid-19. From a scriptural point of view, especially the Hebrew Bible, God is "passible," he feels our pain but he transcends it. The argument of *Fratelli Tutti* is that natural evil, such as Covid-19 is part of God's plan to renew and transform the earth and humanity and we can play our part through solidarity or fraternity and social friendship. In fact, to say it is part of the plan is callous. I think Denis Edwards expresses it better, it is the "the cost of evolution" (Edwards 2006a; 2006b and 2019). It is the conviction that suffering and natural evil exist but God suffers in solidarity with creation and humanity all along the way. They are "the costs of evolution" (Edwards 2006a; 2006b and 2019) but at the end of the day, they will cooperate with the creator in the transformation of creation and humanity. The lesson of Calvary is not the triumph of evil but the triumph of love.

8. Natural Evil, Suffering, the Cost of Evolution and the Christic Omega Point

At the risk of opening a theological Pandora's Box but since I have already connected natural evil, such as Covid-19, suffering and cosmic evolution, I might as well rope in a priest-scientist, Pierre Teilhard de Chardin (1881–1955) who brought evolution to its logical Christological conclusion: Omega Point. Whatever pangs creation may be going through, in the words of St Paul, it is part of the cost of evolution towards its highest point — the Omega Point. Pierre Teilhard de Chardin believed at the time that evolution was *anathema* in the Catholic Church that creation is on a march towards its final point of unification. The Omega Point was effectively the Johannine *Logos*, namely Christ, who, in Johannine terminology was drawing all things to himself. I think the reading "And I, when I am lifted up from the earth, will draw all things to myself" must be preferred to "And I, when I am lifted up from the earth, will draw all people to myself" (John 12.32 *NRSV*).[30] This was the same *Logos* who in the words of the Nicene Creed [Σύμβολον τῆς Νικαίας], was "God from God" [Θεὸν ἐκ Θεοῦ], "Light from Light" [Φῶς ἐκ Φωτός], "True God from true God" [Θεὸν ἀληθινὸν ἐκ Θεοῦ ἀληθινοῦ], and "through him all things were made" [γεννηθέντα οὐ ποιηθέντα]. This is the same *Logos* who describes himself three times in the book of Revelation as "the Alpha and the Omega, the beginning and the end" (Rev 1.8; 21.6 and 22.13). This is what Pierre Teilhard de Chardin says of the Omega. "If we left any contribution or support from Revelation, the only conclusion we could deduce from the existence, once that is accepted, of Omega is that the tide of consciousness of which we form a part is not produced simply by some impulse that originates in ourselves. It feels the pull of a star, upon which, individually and as one whole, we are completing in one union in our process of interiorization. The layers of the world around us take on a vastly richer and more penetrating radiance when they are seen in the context of a Christic-type creation (one, that is, in which a divine involution steps down to combine with the mounting evolution of the cosmos)" (Teilhard de Chardin 1948: 190–191). This Christic Omega point is in the language of Apocalypse, the new heaven and new earth. "Then I saw a new heaven and a new earth; for the first heaven and the first earth had passed away, and the sea was no more" (Rev 21.1 *NRSV*). It is truly a new world order in a much deeper sense than intended or understood by Woodrow Wilson's "new order of the world."[31]

9. *Fratelli Tutti*, Catholic Social Teaching, Covid-19 and a New World Order

Fratelli Tutti [Brothers all] is described as a social encyclical. Social encyclicals, according to the "Social Encyclicals" entry in *Encyclopedia of Catholic Social Thought, Social Science, and Social Policy* are a "large-scale, detailed letter sent out by the Pope to everyone in the world, treating social issues (usually economic ones) with a combination of critique and counsel, defining paramount principles, pointing out urgent problems suggesting a direction for solutions" (Coulter 2007: 978). They often address oppression, the role of the state, subsidiarity, social organisation, concern for social, global and planetary justice, and issues of wealth distribution [distributism]. The foundations of Catholic Social Teaching [*CST*] are widely considered to have been laid by

Pope Leo XIII's 1891 encyclical letter *Rerum Novarum*, which advocated economic distributism. Distributism is an economic theory which asserts that the world's resources and wealth should be widely owned and shared rather than concentrated in the hands of a few. It is now associated with the principles of Catholic social teaching, especially the teachings of Pope Leo XIII in his encyclical *Rerum Novarum* (1891) mentioned above and Pope Pius XI in *Quadragesimo anno* (1931). Distributism views both *laissez-faire* Capitalism, epitomised by the countries of the so-called developed global North, and state socialism, at one time associated with the Union of Soviet Socialist Republics [*USSR*] and Cuba, as equally flawed and exploitative. Distributism favoured economic mechanisms such as cooperatives and member-owned mutual organisations as well as small businesses and large-scale competition law reform such as antitrust laws. As Holger Bonus says, "By agreeing to set up an enterprise of their own through which transactions are made, the members of a cooperative internalize crucial transactions and escape threats to the quasi-rent to the quasi-rent of their investments by outside opportunists. The *benefits of collective organization*, then, (and thus the centripetal force that ties the cooperative together), consist in utilizing transaction-specific assets without depending on outside companies, which potentially could jeopardize the quasi-rent of their investments" (Bonus 1986: 334 — italics in the original). According to Alexandra Twin, "Antitrust laws are regulations that monitor the distribution of economic power in business, making sure that healthy competition is allowed to flourish and economies can grow. Antitrust laws apply to nearly all industries and sectors, touching every level of business, including manufacturing, transportation, distribution, and marketing."[32]

The roots of both Catholic Social Teaching in general and distributism in particular can be traced to the writings of Catholic thinkers such as Thomas Aquinas and Augustine of Hippo, and are also derived from concepts present in the Bible and the cultures of the ancient Near East from which the Bible grew. St John Paul II pointed out in his 1999 Apostolic Exhortation, *Ecclesia in America*, that through "social doctrine, the Church makes an effective contribution to the issues presented by the current globalised economy" and quoted the Synod of Bishops, Second Extraordinary General Assembly, Final Report *Ecclesia sub Verbo Dei Mysteria Christi Celebrans pro Salute Mundi* (December 7, 1985) which declared in its *Propositio* 74 that the moral vision of the Church, expressed in its social doctrine "rests on the threefold cornerstone of human dignity, solidarity and subsidiarity." Just to confirm that for the current encyclical, human dignity is mentioned 9 times (par 22, 25, 37, 125, 127, 168, 207, 268 and 277) solidarity, 20 times (par 11, 36, 75, 114x3, 115, 116x4, 127, 132, 138, 146x2, 152, 168, 169, 187, 205x2, 243, 249) and subsidiarity 3 times (par 142, 175 and 187).

For Pope Francis, Catholic social teaching, "has underscored the error of the neoliberal dogma which holds that the economic and moral orders are so completely distinct from one another that the former is in no way dependent on the latter."[33] He said this on 8 October 2020 when he spoke to representatives of *Moneyval*, the Council of Europe's anti-money laundering watchdog, who were in Rome conducting an annual review of the Vatican, following a year of money-related scandals. "In light of the present circumstances, it would seem that the worship of the ancient golden calf has returned in a new and ruthless guise in the idolatry of money and the dictatorship of an impersonal economy lacking a truly human purpose," he said, insisting that "financial speculation fundamentally aimed at quick profit continues to wreak havoc."[34]

The new social encyclical is inspired by the Pope's namesake, St Francis' *Admonition* VI[35] and is the first encyclical to be signed outside Rome. It was signed on 3 October 2020 at the tomb of St Francis in Assisi. It was then officially released on 4 October 2020 after the midday *Angelus* at the Vatican in Rome. As Junno Arocho Esteves of *Catholic News Service* wrote on 4 October 2020, "At the Vatican's Oct. 4 presentation of the encyclical, *Fratelli Tutti, on Fraternity and Social Friendship*, [Pietro] Parolin, Vatican secretary of state, said the document shows that 'fraternity is not a trend or a fashion which develops over time or at a particular time, but rather is the result of concrete acts.'"[36] Fraternity must be in our DNA. Clearly, the lengths that some people went to during Covid-19 must underscore Pietro Parolin's words.

The original language of the encyclical is Spanish, the Pope's native tongue, which was then translated into the main European languages, German, Portuguese, Italian, French, Polish as well as Arabic. Apart from English, I have also consulted the Italian, Spanish, Portuguese and French translations for this summary. The full title of the encyclical in English is "Encyclical Letter *Fratelli Tutti* of the Holy Father Francis on the Fraternity and Social Friendship." The definite article on "fraternity" was probably not as necessary in English as it was in the Latin languages. An encyclical is the highest classification of any papal document but my experience in the Catholic Church is that encyclicals rarely get to reach the ordinary Christian in the pew. This encyclical — the third of his 7-year-old pontificate — is Francis' diagnosis of the social problems plaguing our world as well as his proposed prognosis which are the fruit of prayer and reflection. Pope Francis started writing the encyclical long before Covid-19 "erupted" as he says but once the ever-new pandemic was in full flow it managed to change and give more impetus to his message about a new world order. As Austen Ivereigh points out, "Although he did not pen *Fratelli tutti* in response to the COVID-19 crisis, the virus hovers over its first chapter, in which he grimly surveys a world sliding back into fragmentation, egotism, and polarization, incapable of the consensus needed to cope with the challenge. But the encyclical was conceived in response to a much broader crisis in modernity, not just the pandemic, and it is on the persuasiveness of its diagnosis and prescription that it will be judged."[37]

i. Fraternity [*Fraternidad*], Social Friendship [*Amistad Social*] and *Fratelli Tutti*

According to Isabella Piro, writing for the *Vatican News*, "What are the great ideals but also the tangible ways to advance for those who wish to build a more just and fraternal world in their ordinary relationships, in social life, politics and institutions? This is mainly the question that '*Fratelli tutti*' is intended to answer: the Pope describes it as a 'Social Encyclical' which borrows the title of the 'Admonitions' of Saint Francis of Assisi, who used these words to 'address his brothers and sisters and proposed to them a way of life marked by the flavour of the Gospel' [*Fratelli Tutti* 2020: par 1].[38] The Encyclical aims at promoting universal fraternity [Spanish:

Fraternidad] and social friendship [Spanish: *Amistad Social*]. In the background of the Encyclical is the Covid-19 pandemic which, Francis reveals, "unexpectedly erupted" as he "was writing this letter." But the global health emergency has helped demonstrate that "no one can face life in isolation" and that the time has truly come to "dream, then, as a single human family" in which we are "brothers and sisters all" [*Fratelli Tutti* 2020: par 8]. It is in this sense that this section is entitled, "New Bottles for New Wine: A New World Order 'Thanks' to Covid-19

ii. The Most Important Encyclical of St Francis' Pontificate

John Allen goes so far as to opine that *Fratelli Tutti* contains "three reasons why it looms as potentially the most important document of this papacy."[39] Firstly, "this is his chance to present his thinking in a comprehensive, orderly, and fully formed way" on the socio-economic, cultural and political devastation of Covid-19. This includes an important interview the Pope gave to a Spanish magazine *Vida Nueva* mentioned above. If the Pope has any axe to grind, it is the global economic injustice, the bane of Catholic social teaching.

Secondly, "although it's a hackneyed cliché to say that the world stands at a crossroads, the world nevertheless stands at a crossroads vis-à-vis the vision Pope Francis has been trying to lay out for the last eight years." Thirdly, "Pope Francis recently sent shock waves through the Vatican by firing Italian Cardinal Angelo Becciu, the former 'substitute' in the Secretariat of State and a man long seen as the embodiment of the place's old guard"[40] sending a message that when it comes to corruption, there are no Vatican sacred cows. The Pope understands well the Gospel maxim, "Why do you take out a speck from your brother."

iii. Brief Overview of the Encyclical *Fratelli Tutti*

The encyclical is divided into 8 chapters (Spanish subtitles are in square brackets): Introduction (par 1–8), Chapter 1: Dark clouds cover the world (par 9–55) [*Las Sombras de un Mundo Cerrado*], Chapter 2: A stranger on the road (par 56–86) [*Un Extrano en el Camino*], Chapter 3: Envisaging and engendering an open world (par 87–127) [*Pensar y Gestar un Mundo Abierto*], Chapter 4: A heart open to the world (par 128–153) [*Un Corazón Abierto al Mundo Entero*], Chapter 5: A better kind of politics (par 154–197) [*La Mejor Polítca*], Chapter 6: Dialogue and friendship in society (par 198–224) [*Diálogo y Amistad Social*], Chapter 7: Paths of renewed encounter (par 225–270) [*Caminos de Reencuentro*] and Chapter 8: Religions at the service of fraternity in our world (271–287) [*Las Religiones al Servicio de la Fraternidad en el Mundo*].[41] Given the convergence of themes, it would be remiss if I did not give a brief summary of the chapters of *Fratelli Tutti* just listed.

Chapter 1, "Dark Clouds over a Closed World," paints a dire global picture replete with manipulation and misunderstanding of concepts such as democracy, freedom, justice; the loss of meaning of social community and history; selfishness and indifference toward the common good; the prevalence of a market logic based on profit and the culture of waste; unemployment, racism, poverty; the disparity of rights and its aberrations such as slavery, trafficking, women subjugated and then forced to abort, organ trafficking etc. Quite clearly, this is a lethal cocktail of a dysfunctional world requiring drastic solutions. In the context of a post Covid-19 era, there cannot be any return to business as usual.

Chapter 2, "A stranger on the road" is dedicated to the figure of the Good Samaritan (Luke 10.25–37). In it, the Pope emphasizes that in an unhealthy society such as ours — what Peter Morrall has referred to as "Insane Society" (Morrall 2020) — that turns its back on suffering and is "illiterate" in caring for the frail and vulnerable. It needs to be converted and practice what St Paul calls *agathōsýnē*[42] in Gal 5.22 — meaning, inherently good, intrinsic goodness (especially as a unique quality and condition); as relating to believers, the goodness that comes from God and showing itself in spiritual, moral excellence. Chapter 2 reminds us that we are in an era in which we are all called to become neighbours to others by "our call to love, one that transcends all prejudices, all historical and cultural barriers, and all petty interests" (*Fratelli Tutti* 2020: par 83). For the Pope, we are co-responsible in creating a society that is inclusive, integrative and uplifting "those who have fallen" by the wayside or are suffering. Such acts of love build bridges because "we were made for love" (*Fratelli Tutti* 2020: par 88).

Chapter 3, "Envisaging and engendering an open world," exhorts us to go "outside the self" — to be missionary — in order to find "a fuller existence in another" (*Ibid*), opening ourselves up to the other according to the dynamism of charity which makes us tend toward "universal fulfilment" (*Fratelli Tutti* 2020: par 95). This call to an open world is made in the light of the plight of migrants forced to flee war-torn areas such as Syria or simply migrants, in South America, fleeing brutal dictatorships. Their efforts are often met by countries closed to migrants. Countries, such as the United Kingdom, once marked by the commonwealth spirit of openness are now become insular.

Chapter 4, "A heart open to the whole world" focuses on those fleeing from war, persecution, natural catastrophes, unscrupulous trafficking, and those who are ripped from their communities of origin. This chapter spells out the principles of chapter 3 driven by the dynamism of charity. The Pope reiterates the constant message of his pontificate epitomised in the ministry of his Almoner, Cardinal Konrad Krajewski, that migrants are to be welcomed, protected, supported and integrated. But the Pope introduces an important caveat that unnecessary migration — mainly and purely for economic advancement — needs to be avoided by creating concrete opportunities to live in dignity in the countries of origin.

Chapter 5, "A better kind of politics" represents one of the most valuable expressions of charity because it is placed at the service of the common good (*Fratelli Tutti* 2020: par 180) and recognises the importance of people, understood as an open category, available for discussion and dialogue (*Fratelli Tutti* 2020: par 160). This is the populism indicated by Francis, which counters that "populism" which ignores the legitimacy of the notion of "people" by attracting consensuses in order to exploit them for its own service and fomenting selfishness in order to increase its own popularity (*Fratelli Tutti* 2020: par 159). But a better politics is also one that protects work, an "essential dimension of social life" (*Fratelli Tutti* 2020: par 162). In Zambia, in the light of the 2021 General Elections, we are in dire need of "a better kind of politics." The Church in Zambia can help the nation to spell out what "a better kind of politics" might look like by election time in 2021 — a better kind of politics that disavows *ochlocracy* or mob rule, the rule of government by a mass of unruly, uncouth and unelected people and the intimidation of the citizenry by largely illiterate party cadres at the behest of the head of state who is effectively the Cadre-in-Chief.

Chapter 6, "Dialogue and friendship in society" is for me, the meat in the sandwich. It proposes solutions to the dreary picture painted in chapter one. The Pope introduces the concept of life as the "art of encounter" (*Fratelli Tutti* 2020: par 215), quoting Vinicius de Moraes' *Samba da Benção*. Marcus Vinícius da Cruz e Mello Moraes (19 October 1913 – 9 July 1980), to give him his full set names was nicknamed *O Poetinha* (The little poet). Along with frequent collaborator Antônio Carlos Jobim, his lyrics and compositions were part of the birth of *bossa nova* [new trend or new wave] music. He recorded several albums and also served as a diplomat. The Pope is indebted to him for the use of the phrase "Life, for all its confrontations, is the art of encounter" [Portuguese: *A vida é a arte do encontro, embora haja tanto desencontro na vida*] cited in the encyclical (*Fratelli Tutti* 2020: par 215). There is an intended pan on "encounter" [*encontro*] and "confrontations" [*desencontro*] lost in translation. It is maintained in the Spanish original, as is to be expected, *encuentro* and *desencuentro*.

For the Pope, this is an encounter with everyone, even with those on the world's peripheries, because "each of us can learn something from others. No one is useless and no one is expendable" (*Fratelli Tutti* 2020: par 215). Then, of particular note, is the Pope's reference to the miracle of "kindness." The Spanish word translated as "kindness" is "*amabilidad*" while the French has "*bienveillance*." A better English translation of "*amabilidad*" is amiability. The French "*bienveillance*" meaning benevolence, is closer to the intended significance of *amabilidad* than kindness. This is an attitude to be recovered because it is a star "shining in the midst of darkness" and "frees us from the cruelty that at times infects human relationships, from the anxiety that prevents us from thinking of others, from the frantic flurry of activity that forgets that others also have a right to be happy" in the contemporary era (*Fratelli Tutti* 2020: par 222–224).

Chapter 7, "Paths of Renewed Encounter," reiterates the value and promotion of peace by underscoring that peace is connected to truth, justice and mercy. Far from the desire for vengeance, it is "proactive" and aims at forming a society based on service to others and on the pursuit of reconciliation and mutual development (*Fratelli Tutti* 2020: par 227–229) citing the example of the Truth and Reconciliation Commission of South Africa (cf. *Fratelli Tutti* 2020: par 229). Thus, peace is an "art" that involves and regards everyone and in which each one must do his or her part in "a never-ending task" (*Fratelli Tutti* 2020: par 232). Forgiveness is linked to peace: we must love everyone, without exception.

Chapter 8, "Religions at the service of fraternity in our world," emphasizes that terrorism is not due to religion but to erroneous interpretations of religious texts, as well as "policies linked to hunger, poverty, injustice, oppression" (*Fratelli Tutti* 2020: par 282–283). This journey of peace among religions is possible and that it is therefore necessary to guarantee religious freedom, a fundamental human right for all believers (*Fratelli Tutti* 2020: par 279). Critics, no doubt, will cite the fate of the underground Church in China as a case in point.

The Pope, for his part quotes the Grand Imam Ahmad Al-Tayyeb, 5 times in the encyclical, together with whom they declared "that religions must never incite war, hateful attitudes, hostility and extremism, nor must they incite violence or the shedding of blood. These tragic realities are the consequence of a deviation from religious teachings. They result from a political manipulation of religions and from interpretations made by religious groups who, in the course of history, have taken advantage of the power of religious sentiment in the hearts of men and women… God, the Almighty, has no need to be defended by anyone and does not want his name to be used to terrorise people" (*Fratelli Tutti* 2020: par 285). The Pope was citing from the "Document on Human Fraternity for World Peace and Living Together."[43] Michael Sean Winters rightly asks, "If this pandemic does not shake us out of our post-modern cultural and moral and spiritual lethargy, what will? Pope Francis is throwing the Catholic Church and the whole world a lifeline. Will we grab it?"[44]

iv.   Fratelli Tutti in 550 Words

This is a powerful social encyclical, along the same lines as other social encyclicals such as, *Rerum Novarum*: On the Condition of Workers (1891) by Leo XIII, *Quadragesimo Anno*: On the Reconstruction of the Social Order (1931) by Pius XI, *Pacem in Terris*: Peace on Earth (1963) by John XXIII, *Populorum Progressio*: On the Development of People (1967) by Paul VI, *Centesimus Annus*: The Hundredth Anniversary of *Rerum Novarum* (1991) by John Paul II. *Fratelli Tutti* is written in the shadow of rising populist leaders in Europe, the USA and even Africa. Fraternity and social friendship are the ways the Pontiff indicates for building a better, more just and peaceful world, with the contribution of all: people and institutions. With an emphatic confirmation of a 'no' to war, even a just war and to globalised indifference.

For *Fratelli Tutti*, professing faith in God as the creator of all human beings, or even simply recognising that all people possess an inherent dignity, has concrete consequences for how people should treat one another and make decisions in politics, economics and social life. Research Professor, Kevin Irwin, former dean of the School of Theology and Religious Studies from 2005–2011 at the Catholic University of America, wrote an introduction to the Paulist Press publication of Pope Francis' latest encyclical, *Fratelli tutti* in which he said, *inter alia*, "*Fratelli tutti* is a fulsome document written in an invitational style. Nevertheless, be prepared for an unremitting invitation to nothing less than a conversion of life in light of Pope Francis' astute assessment of the brokenness and polarisation of today's world."[45]

18

The encyclical decries the scandal of rampant personal, societal and institutional individualism. Instead, he enjoins the need for religious bodies to come together in "fraternity and social friendship" in order to witness to counter cultural values. "The Catholic characteristic and challenge — the common good — is cited and explored here in numerous ways."[46] If I might add, the phrase "common good" is cited 34 times (par 12, 15, 22, 63, 66, 67, 98, 105, 108, 143, 153, 154, 159, 172, 174, 175, 178, 179, 180, 182, 190, 202, 205, 221, 228, 230, 232, 252, 257, 260, 262, 276 and 282) and clearly a favourite *leitmotif* of this important social encyclical.

There is a long tradition of "just war" theory in Catholic theology, including criteria for such a war. I have struggled as a Catholic theologian to defend it. Pope Francis rejects it, arguing that "it is very difficult nowadays to invoke the rational criteria elaborated in earlier centuries to speak of the possibility of a 'just war'" (*Fratelli Tutti* 2020: par 258). The Pope adds an endnote, "Saint Augustine, who forged a concept of 'just war' that we no longer uphold in our own day, also said that 'it is a higher glory still to stay war itself with a word, than to slay men with the sword, and to procure or maintain peace by peace, not by war.'"[47] This important position seems to have escaped early commentators on the encyclical.

10. Africa Welcomes *Fratelli Tutti*

On 6 October 2020, two days after the release of *Fratelli Tutti*, Cardinal Philippe Ouédraogo of Ouagadougou, Burkina Faso, President of the Symposium of Episcopal Conferences of Africa and Madagascar (*SECAM*), thanked Pope Francis for this encyclical, saying it urges people everywhere toward a "renewed commitment to universal brotherhood, friendship, solidarity and peaceful co-existence."[48] "In view of the current coronavirus pandemic, which has established that no one can face life in isolation; that we are a single human family and true brothers and sisters of the one Father, God, the call invites for swift response."[49] In March 2020 Cardinal Philippe Ouédraogo tested positive for the coronavirus. After his recovery, he appealed for bilateral and multilateral aid agencies to offer greater solidarity with Africa, which he said lacks the resources and health and safety kits to fight the pandemic. In his recent statement, the Cardinal reiterated Pope Francis's call in *Fratelli Tutti* to intensify efforts aimed at fostering "true brotherhood, solidarity, dialogue, mutual acceptance, trust and support," which he said are "crucial values for our current world visibly divided along cultural, religious, social, political and ideological lines or principles."[50]

11. Five Takeaways from *Fratelli Tutti*

I am picking five major takeaways from this social encyclical. The first two, about the nature of this encyclical, are closely connected: the dark picture of our world (chapter 1) and the required response of a good Samaritan (chapter 2). The third, that there is nothing he says here which is completely new, is no surprise to Pope Francis watchers but it the manner in which what he says is expressed. It is an invitation to what is best for us rather than force-feeding us. This encyclical is vintage Francis and already can be traced to his post-Synod Apostolic exhortation, *Evangelii Gaudium* which is cited 13 times in *Fratelli Tutti*. Another key component of Pope Francis was an

19

Easter reflection he made for the Spanish newspaper *Vida Nueva* entitled *"Un Plan Para Resucitar: Una Meditación*. It is the way he strings his argument which is compelling. Anyone expecting sensational Media soundbites is likely to be disappointed and is the point of my fourth and fifth takeaways. Generally, the soundbite red meat has been avoided with the exception of the gender issue but I am inclined to think the criticism is without merit.

i. The Encyclical is no Quick Read for Partisan Spin

This is a Catholic document, in the sense of universal. There is no point in reading it to pick out proof texts for whatever ideology you hold. But in the same breath, it requires critical reflection and application to one's context. As Thomas Reese rightly points out, *"Fratelli Tutti*, Francis' third encyclical, presents his vision of how humanity must respond to the needs of the 21st century. It will take time to absorb, but it can be life sustaining."[51] Those who want to bicker will do so, as Archbishop Maria Viganò has done, opining that "The Catholic concept of 'freedom of religion' is replaced by the concept of 'religious freedom' theorized by the Second Vatican Council, bartering the divine right of the Church to freedom of worship, preaching and government with the recognition of the right to error to spread not only in general, but even in Christian nations." [52]

ii. The Encyclical is a Heavy Read

Encyclicals are always heavy and often ponderous. They are magisterial documents meant to last the test of time. The reason why *Fratelli Tutti* cannot be a quick read is that it is a heavy read by nature. This is not a read for the beach or on your daily commute to work or the stuff of binge reading. A chapter per reading session may be the recommended minimum digestive speed. I found myself stopping after a short paragraph at a time to ask myself where the Pope was coming from. From a hermeneutical perspective, I tried to check all the endnotes. There was one surprise in store for me: the variety of sources.

The encyclical, some 43,000 words, comes with 288 endnotes. Unlike many papal documents, some of these endnotes are not your usual fair of sources and this is likely to drive Pope Francis' detractors insane. Unusual sources include Charles de Foucauld's *Méditation sur le Notre Père*, even a movie, "Pope Francis: A Man of His Word" by Wim Wenders, Catholic Bishops' Conference of India, "Response of the Church in India to the Present-day Challenges" (9 March 2016), Bishops' Conference of Colombia, *Por el bien de Colombia: diálogo, reconciliación y desarrollo integral* (26 November 2019), Southern African Catholic Bishops' Conference, "Pastoral Letter on Christian Hope in the Current Crisis" (May 1986), Episcopal Conference of the Congo, *Message au Peuple de Dieu et aux femmes et aux hommes de bonne volonté* (9 May 2018), Vinicius de Moraes, *Samba da Benção*, from the recording *Um encontro no Au bon Gourmet*, Rio de Janeiro (2 August 1962), Social Commission of the Bishops of France, *Declaration Réhabiliter la Politique* (17 February 1999), Paul Ricoeur, *Histoire et Verité* (1967), United States Conference of Catholic Bishops, Pastoral Letter Against Racism *Open Wide Our Hearts: The Enduring Call to Love* (November 2018), *Talmud Bavli* (Babylonian Talmud), etc., to mention but a few. The Pope could not have been more universal in outreach. But for his detractors such as Carlo Maria Viganò, the former nuncio to the United States of America, this is obviously a blotting of the Pope's copybook.

iii. The Encyclical is Bergoglio *Redivivus*

The very first words introducing the new Pope on that drizzly Wednesday evening on 13 March 2013 telegraphed that we were in for a surprise. The cardinal proto-deacon, Jean-Louis Tauran made the solemn announcement to the people gathered in St Peter's Square at 8.12 pm from the external loggia of the Hall of Blessings of the Vatican Basilica following the white smoke which occurred at 7.06 pm from the Sistine Chapel, *"Annuntio vobis 21audium magnum; habemus Papam: Eminentissimum ac Reverendissimum Dominum, Dominum Georgium Marium Sanctae Romanae Ecclesiae Cardinalem Bergoglio qui sibi nomen imposuit Franciscum"* [I announce to you great joy; we have a pope: The most eminent and most reverend lord, Lord Jorge Mario Cardinal Bergoglio of the Holy Roman Church who has taken the name Francis].[53] Pope Francis appeared and asked the people to pray for him before he blessed the world, at which point the conclave concluded. The novelty of the encyclical does not lie in what or how the Pope says it but in the connections which he makes, such as the future of our planet and of humanity in the face of Covid-19, by linking it with age-old Catholic social virtues such as fraternity, solidarity and subsidiarity. This is not just Pope Francis speaking. It is also Jorge Mario Bergoglio. One of his regular sources is his first Apostolic Exhortation, *Evangelii Gaudium*. The source of his inspiration for the encyclical, except Francis of Assisi, is unusual and makes his detractors such as Archbishop Carlo Maria Viganò squirm. "In these pages of reflection on universal fraternity, I felt inspired particularly by Saint Francis of Assisi, but also by others of our brothers and sisters who are not Catholics: Martin Luther King, Desmond Tutu, Mahatma Gandhi and many more. Yet I would like to conclude by mentioning another person of deep faith who, drawing upon his intense experience of God, made a journey of transformation towards feeling a brother to all. I am speaking of Blessed Charles de Foucauld" (*Fratelli Tutti* 2020: par 286).

iv. There are no Bombshells in the Encyclical

Anyone looking for Media soundbites of a controversial nature, such as gay rights, will be disappointed. This is not a Media outlet in search of popularity ratings. The Pope says nothing about internal Church politics such as the ordination of married men and the admission of women to holy orders. He mentions abortion only once in passing in connection with criminal networks subjugating "women and then forces them to abort" (*Fratelli Tutti* 2020: par 24). Not even the American battle cry of pro-life gets any mention. There is nothing about *LGBTQ* [Lesbian, Gay, Bi-sexual, Trans-sexual and Queer] persons. I think this is a can of worms not deemed worth opening at this juncture. Not even the famous comments about "who am I to judge?" Pope Francis was responding to questions about whether there was a "gay lobby" in the Vatican when he responded, "If a person is gay and seeks God and has good will, who am I to judge?"[54] We all

21

know how the Media reported that interview. You would be excused for thinking no other topic was dealt with.

Little is said about women, a fact likely to disappoint women's groups. I am not sure whether I share the disappointment. Here are a few stats on the words, woman or women. Woman is mentioned 7 times (par 6, 83x2, 85, 196 and 277) and women, 21 times (par 8, 23x2, 24x3, 55, 67, 104, 121, 136, 157, 193, 194, 221, 225, 227, 274, 277, 285x20. Now, let's compare that with man, 33 times (par 4, 6, 36, 56x2, 57, 59, 63x4, 67, 69, 70, 71, 72x2, 76, 78, 78, 82, 85, 88, 101x2, 150, 196, 222, 240x2, 265, 270x2, 273, 287) and men, 22 times (par 8, 23, 24x2, 54, 67, 104, 136, 157, 193, 194, 221, 225, 246, 247, 265x2, 272, 274, 277, 285x2). Unless one goes through all these occurrences, I am not sure how significant these are but what the Pope does say about women is positive and is in keeping with the tenor of his pontificate: "Similarly, the organisation of societies worldwide is still far from reflecting clearly that women possess the same dignity and identical rights as men. We say one thing with words, but our decisions and reality tell another story. Indeed, 'doubly poor are those women who endure situations of exclusion, mistreatment and violence, since they are frequently less able to defend their rights'" (*Fratelli Tutti* 2020: par 23). The Pope is here quoting his first Apostolic Exhortation *Evangelii Gaudium* (*Evangelium Gaudium* 2013: par 212), in my view still his *opus magnum*. There he says, "Doubly poor are those women who endure situations of exclusion, mistreatment and violence, since they are frequently less able to defend their rights. Even so, we constantly witness among them impressive examples of daily heroism in defending and protecting their vulnerable families." The Pope also condemns violence against women and human trafficking. The encyclical sees men and women as equal partners in dealing with the world's problems. But as one female religious friend of mine of 50 years religious service told me recently, "This will take a long time."

v.   The Encyclical is no Panacea for Solving World's Problems

My fifth and final takeaway is that, although the Pope does make specific proposals, the encyclical is more about attitudes and values that underpin what we do than programmes. Samuel Gregg's critique completely misses this point. In the Pope's meditation on the Good Samaritan, for instance, Pope Francis concludes, "The parable is clear and straightforward, yet it also evokes the interior struggle that each of us experiences as we gradually come to know ourselves through our relationships with our brothers and sisters. Sooner or later, we will all encounter a person who is suffering [or is marginalised]. Today there are more and more of them. The decision to include or exclude those lying wounded along the roadside can serve as a criterion for judging every economic, political, social and religious project. Each day we have to decide whether to be Good Samaritans or indifferent bystanders. And if we extend our gaze to the history of our own lives and that of the entire world, all of us are, or have been, like each of the characters in the parable. All of us have in ourselves something of the wounded man, something of the robber, something of the passers-by, and something of the Good Samaritan" (*Fratelli Tutti* 2020: par 69). In this sense, *Fratelli Tutti* is one gigantic consciousness examen. If we are honest with ourselves we have to admit that our default position seems to be that of bystanders or passers-by to the plight of the many people who fall into the hands of robbers.

12. Conclusion

This article has given a socio-religious or theological perspective on the new encyclical by Pope Francis, *Fratelli Tutti*. Based on three social virtues, fraternity, solidarity and social friendship, the encyclical is a call to humanity to unite and to build a brave new world order after the Covid-19 pandemic. I have limited myself to examining why the encyclical has been well-received (reception of *Fratelli Tutti*), how Covid-19 calls us to a new way of being human (New bottles for new wine and God's passibility in a post Covid-19 Era) in which humanity is being challenged not to return to business as usual in the way we deal with each other; how natural evil, such as a pandemic, cannot thwart the plan of the creator; how the new encyclical, *Fratelli Tutti* factors into a new World Order (*Fratelli Tutti* and a new world order "thanks" to Covid-19) and ending with five lessons I was able to cull from *Fratelli Tutti* (Five takeaways from *Fratelli Tutti*).

This is an encyclical destined to convert our planet and its humanity and per chance lead us to Utopia. As I have noted above, if the world listens to *Fratelli Tutti*, or as my friend Josephine Shamwana-Lungu, in charge of Catholic education in the Archdiocese of Lusaka, Zambia told me recently, if we adopt the "spirit of *Fratelli Tutti*,"[55] surely, "it will be an epochal change."[56] As Raymond de Souza rightly notes, "The recent encyclical of Pope Francis, *Fratelli Tutti* (*FT*), is another literary *behemoth*. Its massive size means that, upon an initial reading, it is not possible to take in all of the specific items covered — from immigration to criminal justice to war and peace. It might be better, then, to situate *FT* broadly in the tradition of Catholic social teaching, in light of the Holy Father's own magisterium and as a response to current global political realities."[57] Criticisms of the encyclical, such as Samuel Gregg's, miss the wood for the trees when he claims that "*Fratelli Tutti* is a familiar mixture of dubious claims, strawmen and genuine insights."[58] This is a macro sermon of *behemoth* proportions on the future of the planet and humanity designed to wake us from our slumber.

References

Bonus, Holger (1986), "The Cooperative Association as a Business Enterprise: A Study in the Economics of Transactions," *Journal of Institutional and Theoretical Economics (JITE)* / *Zeitschrift für die gesamte Staatswissenschaft* 142(2): 310–339

Castillo, Mauricio (2012), "The Omega Point and Beyond: The Singularity Event," *American Journal of Neuroradiology* 33(3): 393–395

Coulter, Michael L, Stephen M. Krason, Richard S. Myers, Joseph A. Varacalli (2007), *Encyclopedia of Catholic Social Thought, Social Science, and Social Policy* [2-Volume Set], Lanham MD: Scarecrow Press

Edwards, Denis (2006a), "Every Sparrow that Falls to the Ground: The Cost of Evolution and the Christ-Event," *Ecotheology* 11(1): 103–123

Edwards, Denis (2006b), "Resurrection and the Costs of Evolution: A Dialogue with Rahner on Noninterventionist Theology," *Theological Studies* 67(4): 816–833

Edwards, Denis (2019), "Sublime Communion and the Costs of Evolution," *Irish Theological Quarterly* 84(1): 22–38

Edwards, James R (2002), *The Gospel According to Mark*, Grand Rapids MI and Cambridge: William B Eerdmans Publishing Company

Gramsci, Antonio (1971), *Selections from the Prison Notebooks of Antonio Gramsci*, trans. and edited by Q. Hoarc and G. Nowdl-Smlth, New York: International Publishers

Huxley, Julian (1950), "New Bottles for New Wine: Ideology and Scientific Knowledge," *The Journal of the Royal Anthropological Institute of Great Britain and Ireland* 80(1/2): 7–23

Longo, Gianfranco (2013), "*Dal Fiat Al Consumatum Est: L'Eucaristico Essere della Creazione, Rinnovata tra Calvario e Resurrezione di Gesù* [From *Fiat* to *Consumatum Est*: The Eucharistic Being of Creation, Renovated Between Calvary and Resurrection of Jesus], *Synesis* 5(1): 16–31

Moltmann, Jürgen (2015), *The Crucified God*, Minneapolis MN: Fortress Press

Morrall, Peter (2020), *Insane Society: A Sociology of Mental Health*, Abingdon and New York: Routledge

Peckham, John C (2012), "The Concept of Divine Love in the Context of the God-World Relationship," *Dissertations* 125, https://digitalcommons.andrews.edu/dissertations/125 [file:///F:/Research/The%20Concept%20of%20Divine%20Love.pdf]

Pope Francis (4 October 2020), Encyclical Letter *Fratelli Tutti* of the Holy Father Francis on the Fraternity and Social Friendship, Vatican City: Editrice Libreria Vaticana

Spivak, Gayatri C (2005), "Scattered Speculations on the Subaltern and the Popular," *Postcolonial Studies* 8: 475–486

Synod of Bishops (7 December 1985), Second Extraordinary General Assembly, Final Report *Ecclesia sub Verbo Dei Mysteria Christi Celebrans pro Salute Mundi*, Vatican City: Editrice Libreria Vaticana

Taliaferro, Charles (1989), "The Passibility of God," *Religious Studies* 25(2): 217–224

Talbot, John Michael, ed (2019), *Francis of Assisi's Sermon on the Mount: Lessons from the Admonitions*, Brewster MA: Paraclete Press

Teilhard de Chardin, Pierre (1948), *Toward the Future*, San Diego, London, New York: Harcourt Inc

Verloo, Mieke (2016), "Subaltern," in: Nancy A. Naples (ed), *The Wiley Blackwell Encyclopedia of Gender and Sexuality Studies*, Cambridge: Wiley-Blackwell

Wilson, Woodrow (9 September 1919), "Address at the University of Minnesota Armory in Minneapolis," Online by Gerhard Peters and John T. Woolley, *The American Presidency Project* https://www.presidency.ucsb.edu/node/317892 (Accessed on 02.12.2020)

About the Author

Tarcisius Mukuka is a biblical exegete by training. His ideal job is research in the Humanities and Social Sciences. He holds a doctorate in Biblical Hermeneutics from the University of Surrey in the United Kingdom. His doctoral dissertation was entitled *Orality as Casualty: Contextual and Postcolonial Analysis of Biblical Hermeneutics in Bembaland* (2014). He is currently a senior lecturer in Religious Studies at Kwame Nkrumah University in Kabwe. He is also President of *Theologians against Violence*, a praxis-oriented think-tank with the immediate aim of contributing to free, fair, transparent and peaceful elections in Zambia; beginning with the 2021 General Elections. His research interests include apocalyptic literature, postcolonialism and the Bible, gender and the Bible, the Bible and Misogyny, religion, politics and power. He is the author of *Spoken Voice/Written Word: Negotiating How We Hear/Read the Bible* (2016) published by Lambert Academic Publishing and *In the Eye of a Very Catholic Storm* (forthcoming), by Crown Arts Publishers.

Endnotes

[1] The English version of "Encyclical Letter *Fratelli Tutti* of the Holy Father Francis on Fraternity and Social Friendship," with provision for the Spanish original, German, Portuguese, Arabic, Polish, Italian and French, is found on, http://www.vatican.va/content/francesco/en/encyclicals/documents/papa-francesco_20201003_enciclica-fratelli-tutti.html (Accessed on 04.10.2020)

[2] Devin Watkins (6 October 2020), "'*Fratelli tutti:*' A radical blueprint for post-Covid world," *Vatican News*, https://www.vaticannews.va/en/church/news/2020-10/reactions-fratelli-tutti-cafod-irish-new-zealand-bishops.html (Accessed on 09.10.2020)

[3] *Ibid.* The phrase "culture of encounter" appears 7 times in *Fratelli Tutti* (par 30x2, 215, 216, 217x2 and 232).

[4] *CAFOD* (2020), "What does *CAFOD* do?" https://cafod.org.uk/ (Accessed on 11.10.2020)

[5] Vinicius de Moraes, *Samba da Benção*, from the recording *Um encontro no Au bon Gourmet*, Rio de Janeiro (2 August 1962)

[6] Devin Watkins (6 October 2020), "'*Fratelli tutti*': A radical blueprint for post-Covid world," *Vatican News*, https://www.vaticannews.va/en/church/news/2020-10/reactions-fratelli-tutti-cafod-irish-new-zealand-bishops.html (Accessed on 09.10.2020)

[7] The Canticle of the Sun or the Canticle of Creatures was the inspiration behind Pope Francis' second encyclical *Laudato Si'*. A text of the canticle can be found on this link, https://www.sacredtexts.com/chr/wosf/wosf22.htm (Accessed on 15.10.2020)

[8] *Christian Life Community* (2020), "Christian Life Community (CLC)," http://www.cvx-clc.net/l-en/aboutUs.html (Accessed on 28.11.2020)

[9] Manuel Martínez Arteaga (2020), Editorial, *Progressio* [Number 1, 2020], page 1

[10] James Bickerton (8 October 2020), "Donald Trump says catching coronavirus was a 'gift from God' after leaving hospital," *Express*, https://www.express.co.uk/news/world/1345127/Coronavirus-news-US-Donald-Trump-COVID-19-White-House-pandemic-remdesivir (Accessed on 08.10.2020)

[11] *World Health Organisation* (2020), "Coronavirus disease (COVID-19) pandemic" https://www.who.int/emergencies/diseases/novel-coronavirus-2019?gclid=EAIaIQobChMI-fuUsuv7AIVAu7tCh0otwmSEAAYASAAEgJTNPD_BwE (Accessed on 12.10.2020)

[12] *Pax Christi* (6 October 2020), "*Fratelli Tutti*: A new encyclical," https://paxchristi.org.uk/2020/10/06/fratelli-tutti-a-new-encyclical/ (Accessed on 14.10.2020)

[13] Gerard O'Connell (13 October 2020), "Cardinal Czerny on 'Fratelli Tutti:' Pope Francis addresses a world 'on the brink,'" *America Magazine*, https://www.americamagazine.org/faith/2020/10/13/cardinal-czerny-interview-fratelli-tutti-pope-francis-encyclical (Accessed on 14.10.2020)

[14] Samuel Gregg (10 October 2020), *"Fratelli Tutti* is a familiar mixture of dubious claims, strawmen, genuine insights," *The Catholic World Report*, https://www.catholicworldreport.com/2020/10/05/fratelli-tutti-is-a-mixture-of-dubious-claims-strawmen-genuine-insights/ (Accessed on 11.10.2020)

[15] *Ibid*

[16] Larry Chapp (9 October 2020), *"Fratelli Tutti* and its critics," *The Catholic World Report*, https://www.catholicworldreport.com/2020/10/09/fratelli-tutti-and-its-critics/ (Accessed on 14.10.2020)

[17] *Ibid*

[18] Carlo Maria Viganò (5 October 2020), "Perché critico l'enciclica *Fratelli Tutti*," *Smart Magazine*, https://www.startmag.it/mondo/perche-critico-enciclica-fratelli-tutti/ (Accessed on 14.10.2020)

[19] Carlo Maria Viganò uses the Italian term *subalternità* [subalternity] in its popularr sense of subordination but in its postcolonial sense it carries the sense of Marxist struggle against hegemonic dominance and is understood positively, especially in its use by Antonio Gramsci. Gayatri Chakravorty Spivak, however, understands it more negatively. As Mieke Verloo writes, "Subaltern as a concept is best understood as related to issues of domination and power, democracy and citizenship, resistance and transformation. According to Gayatri Chakravorty Spivak, subalternity is a position without identity, a position 'where social lines of mobility, being elsewhere, do not permit the formation of a recognizable basis of action' (Spivak 2005: 476)." (Verloo 2016: 1).

[20] Carlo Maria Viganò (5 October 2020), "Perché critico l'enciclica *Fratelli Tutti*," *Smart Magazine*, https://www.startmag.it/mondo/perche-critico-enciclica-fratelli-tutti/ (Accessed on 14.10.2020)

[21] See endnote 17 above.

[22] Eugenio Scalfari (1 October 2013), "The Pope: how the Church will change," *La Republicca*, https://www.repubblica.it/cultura/2013/10/01/news/pope_s_conversation_with_scalfari_english-67643118/, accessed on 14.10.2020. The original interview was in Italian, "Papa Francesco a Scalfari: così cambierò la Chiesa," https://www.repubblica.it/cultura/2013/10/01/news/papa_francesco_a_scalfari_cos_cambier_la_chiesa-67630792/ (Accessed on 16.10.2020)

[23] *Ibid*. I have touched up the translation for syntactical and translational accuracy.

[24] Josephine Shamwana-Lungu (13 October 2020), telephone conversation

[25] Eugenio Scalfari (1 October 2013), "The Pope: how the Church will change," *La Repubblica*, https://www.repubblica.it/cultura/2013/10/01/news/pope_s_conversation_with_scalfari_english-67643118/ (Accessed on 14.10.2020)

[26] *BBC* News (6 June 2014), "Pope Francis replaces Vatican financial watchdog board," https://www.bbc.com/news/business-27727304 (Accessed on 14.10.2020)

[27] Claire Giangravé (8 September 2020), "Pope Francis launches his post-COVID agenda with announcement of new encyclical," *Religion News Service*, https://religionnews.com/2020/09/08/pope-francis-launches-his-post-covid-agenda-with-announcement-of-new-encyclical/ (Accessed on 12.10.2020)

[28] Papa Francisco (17 April 2020), *"Un Plan Para Resucitar: Una Meditación,"* *Vida Nueva*, https://www.vidanuevadigital.com/wp-content/uploads/2020/04/UN-PLAN-PARA-RESUCITAR-PAPA-FRANCISCO-VIDA-NUEVA.pdf (Accessed on 29.09.2020)

[29] *Ibid*.

[30] The Greek text reads, "κἀγὼ ἐὰν ὑψωθῶ ἐκ τῆς γῆς, πάντας ἑλκύσω πρὸς ἐμαυτόν" [And when I should be lifted up from the earth, I will draw all to myself]. Most commentators conclude that since πάντας is accusative masculine plural, it must be referring to people. I suggest it was an intentional ellipsis capable of including people and the entire cosmos personified.

[31] Woodrow Wilson (9 September 1919), "Address at the University of Minnesota Armory in Minneapolis," Online by Gerhard Peters and John T. Woolley, *The American Presidency Project* https://www.presidency.ucsb.edu/node/317892 (Accessed on 02.12.2020)

[32] Alexandra Twin (7 October 2020), "Antitrust," *Investopedia,* https://www.investopedia.com/terms/a/antitrust.asp#:~:text=The%20trust%20in%20antitrust%20refers,an d%20give%20consumers%20more%20options (Accessed on 09.10.2020)

[33] Elise Ann Allen (8 October 2020), "As Vatican faces financial review, pope condemns 'idolatry' of neoliberal economy," *Crux*, https://cruxnow.com/vatican/2020/10/as-vatican-faces-financial-review-pope-condemns-idolatry-of-neoliberal-economy/ (Accessed on 08.10.2020)

[34] *Ibid*

[35] *Admonition* 6, 1, "Let us all, brothers, consider the Good Shepherd who, to save His sheep, bore the suffering of the Cross. The sheep of the Lord followed Him in tribulation and persecution and shame, in hunger and thirst, in infirmity and temptations and in all other ways; and for these things they have received everlasting life from the Lord. Wherefore it is a great shame for us, the servants of God that, whereas the Saints have practised works, we should expect to receive honour and glory for reading and preaching the same" (Talbot 2019: 59).

[36] Junno Arocho Esteves (4 October 2020), "Encyclical highlights need for fraternity to counter war, cardinal says," *Crux*, https://cruxnow.com/vatican/2020/10/catholic-church-encyclical-encyclicals-fratelli-tutti-pope-francis-vatican/ (Accessed on 06.10.2020)

[37] Austen Ivereigh (4 October 2020), "Pope Francis' Call to Fraternity: The making of '*Fratelli tutti,*'" *Commonweal*, https://www.commonwealmagazine.org/pope-franciss-call-fraternity (Accessed on 18.10.2020)

[38] Isabella Piro (4 October 2020), "'*Fratelli tutti:*' Long summary of Pope Francis' Social Encyclical," *Vatican News*, https://www.vaticannews.va/en/pope/news/2020-10/fratelli-tutti-pope-fraternity-social-friendship-long-summary.html (Accessed on 09.10.2020)

[39] John L Allen (3 October 2020), "As Pope named 'Francis' heads to Assisi, a lot rides on new encyclical," *Crux*, https://cruxnow.com/news-analysis/2020/10/as-pope-named-francis-heads-to-assisi-a-lot-rides-on-new-encyclical/ (Accessed on 04.10.2020)

[40] *Ibid*

[41] Pope Francis (4 October 2020), Encyclical Letter *Fratelli Tutti* of the Holy Father Francis On the Fraternity and Social Friendship, http://www.vatican.va/content/francesco/en/encyclicals/documents/papafrancesco_20201003_enciclica-fratelli-tutti.html (Accessed on 04.10.2020)

[42] Cf. Gal 5.22 *NRSV*, "By contrast, the fruit of the Spirit is love, joy, peace, patience, kindness, generosity, faithfulness." *Agathōsýnē* means inherently good or intrinsic goodness (especially as a unique quality and condition; as relating to believers, it is the goodness that comes from God and showing itself in spiritual and moral excellence. The *NRSV* translates as generosity.

[43] Pope Francis, Grand Imam Ahmad Al-Tayyeb (2019), "Document on Human Fraternity for World Peace and Living Together," Abu Dhabi (4 February 2019): *L'Osservatore Romano*, 4–5 February 2019, p. 6

[44] Michael Sean Winters (4 October 2020), "'*Fratelli Tutti*' challenges our country and our Church," *National Catholic Reporter*, https://www.ncronline.org/news/opinion/distinctly-catholic/fratelli-tutti-challenges-our-country-and-our-church (Accessed on 04.10.2020)

[45] Kevin W. Irwin (4 October 2020), "*Fratelli tutti*: 'Don't just read it, pray it'" *Vatican News*, https://www.vaticannews.va/en/pope/news/2020-10/fratelli-tutti-encyclical-kevin-irwincommentary.html (Accessed on 06.10.2020)

[46] *Ibid*

[47] *Fratelli Tutti* (2020), Endnote 242 cf. *Epistola* 229, 2 in: *PL* 33, 1020

[48] Elise Ann Allen (9 October 2020), "African bishops call for 'swift response' to new encyclical," *Crux*, https://cruxnow.com/church-in-africa/2020/10/african-bishops-call-for-swift-response-to-new-encyclical/ (Accessed on 10.10.2020)

[49] *Ibid*

[50] *Ibid*

[51] Thomas Reese (4 October 2020), "Five things to look for in Pope Francis' new encyclical, '*Fratelli Tutti*'" *Religion News Service*, https://religionnews.com/2020/10/04/five-things-to-look-for-in-new-papal-encyclical-fratelli-tutti/ (Accessed on 10.10.2020)

[52] Carlo Maria Viganò (4 October 2020), "*Monsignor Viganò: 'Dimensione soprannaturale totalmente assente. Imbarazzante la falsificazione di san Francesco. Sconcertante l'appiattimento sul pensiero unico mondialista'*" https://www.aldomariavalli.it/2020/10/04/ecco-fratelli-tutti-manifesto-sociale-di-francesco-con-un-commento-di-monsignor-vigano/ (Accessed on 06.10.2020)

[53] *Sala Stampa della Santa Sede* (13 March 2020), "*L'annuncio dell'elezione del Papa*," *Bolletino*, https://press.vatican.va/content/salastampa/it/bollettino/pubblico/2013/03/13/0147.pdf (Accessed on 08.10.2020)

[54] *BBC* News (29 July 2013), "Pope Francis: Who am I to judge gay people?" https://www.bbc.com/news/worldeurope23489702#:~:text=Pope%20Francis%20has%20said%20gay,marginalised%20but%20integrated%20into%20society.&text=%22If%20a%20person%20is%20gay,they%20could%20not%20be%20priests (Accessed on 13.10.2020)

[55] Josephine Shamwana-Lungu (3 October 2020), telephone conversation

[56] Eugenio Scalfari (1 October 2013), "The Pope: how the Church will change," *La Repubblica*, https://www.repubblica.it/cultura/2013/10/01/news/pope_s_conversation_with_scalfari_english-67643118/ (Accessed on 14.10.2020)

[57] Raymond J. de Souza (9 October 2020), "'*Fratelli Tutti*:' Pope Francis' Response to Current Global Political Realities," *National Catholic Register*, https://www.ncregister.com/commentaries/fratelli-tutti-pope-francis-response-to-current-global-political-realities (Accessed on 11.10.2020)

[58] Samuel Gregg (10 October 2020), "*Fratelli Tutti* is a familiar mixture of dubious claims, strawmen, genuine insights," *The Catholic World Report*, https://www.catholicworldreport.com/2020/10/05/fratelli-tutti-is-a-mixture-of-dubious-claims-strawmen-genuine-insights/ (Accessed on 11.10.2020)